Thank you for purcha _ _ _ _ _ _ , _ _ _ _
powerful quotes give you the inspiration you need to
succeed in whatever endeavor you find yourself in
the middle of.

For even more inspiration check out our collection of
eye-catching typography artwork. Our museum-
quality posters and hand-stretched canvas prints
make a statement in any room while featuring one of
our hand-picked inspirational quotes.

www.QuotesThatInspire.me

Impossible is not a fact. It's an opinion. Impossible is not a declaration. It's a dare. Impossible is potential. Impossible is temporary. Impossible is nothing."

– Muhammad Ali

It's not whether you get
knocked down, it's whether you
get up. ~

Vince Lombardi

~

*If you want to be the best, you
have to do things that other
people aren't willing to do.*

-Michael Phelps

You are never a loser
until you quit
trying.

\- Mike Ditka

~

There may be people that have more talent than you, but there's no excuse for anyone to work harder than you do.

\- Derek Jeter

It's hard to beat a person
who never gives up.

- Babe Ruth

~

Pain is temporary. It may last
a minute, or an hour, or a day,
or a year, but eventually it will
subside and something else
will take its place. If I quit,
however, it lasts forever.

–Lance Armstrong

It is not the size of a man but the size of his heart that matters

–Evander Holyfield

~

I've missed more than 9,000 shots in my career. I've lost almost 300 games. 26 times, I've been trusted to take the game winning shot and missed. I've failed over and over and over again in my life. And that is why I succeed

–Michael Jordan

You miss 100 percent of the shots you don't take –

Wayne Gretzky

~

IF YOU THINK YOU CAN'T, YOU WON'T, AND

IF YOU THINK YOU CAN, YOU WILL.

—KELLIE WELLS

You have to believe in yourself when no one else does.

—Venus Williams

~

Talented players don't always succeed. Some don't even make the team. It's more what's inside

-Brett Favre

A catcher must want to catch. He must make up his mind that it isn't the terrible job it is painted, and that he isn't going to say every day, 'Why, oh why with so many other positions in baseball did I take up this one.'

-Bill Dickey

Every day, we've got to do something physical. It's mind, body and spirit.

-Ray Lewis

~

The most rewarding things you do in life are often the ones that look like they cannot be done.

-Arnold Palmer

Success isn't measured by money or power or social rank. Success is measured by your discipline and inner peace.

-Mike Ditka

~

I've always made a total effort, even when the odds seemed entirely against me. I never quit trying; I never felt that I didn't have a chance to win.

-Arnold Palmer

You have to do something in your life that is honorable and not cowardly if you are to live in peace with yourself.

-Larry Brown

~

I didn't believe in team motivation. I believe in getting a team prepared so it knows it will have the necessary confidence when it steps on the field and be prepared to play a good game.

-Tom Landry

To me, football is so much about mental toughness, it's digging deep, it's doing whatever you need to do to help a team win and that comes in a lot of shapes and forms.

-Tom Brady

~

Practice, work hard, and give it everything you have.

-Dizzy Dean

My attitude is that if you push me towards something that you think is a weakness, then I will turn that perceived weakness into a strength.

-Michael Jordan

~

I think about baseball when I wake up in the morning. I think about it all day and I dream about it at night. The only time I don't think about it is when I'm playing it.

-Carl Yastrzemski

For an athlete, there's no time off... until it's over.

-Terry Bradshaw

~

I want winners. I want people who want to win.

-Mike Singletary

Never die easy. Why run out of bounds and die easy? Make that linebacker pay. It carries into all facets of your life. It's okay to lose, to die, but don't die without trying, without giving it your best.

-Walter Payton

~

THE MOST PREPARED ARE THE MOST DEDICATED.

-RAYMOND BERRY

Baseball was, is and always will be to me the best game in the world.

-Babe Ruth

~

If you train hard, you'll not only be hard, you'll be hard to beat.

-Herschel Walker

Make sure your worst enemy doesn't live between your own two ears.

–Laird Hamilton

~

Never let your head hang down. Never give up and sit down and grieve. Find another way.

-Satchel Paige

If you're successful in what you do over a period of time, you'll start approaching records, but that's not what you're playing for. You're playing to challenge and be challenged.-

Lou Brock

~

Don't look back. Something might be gaining on you.

-Satchel Paige

You must also give mental and physical fitness priority.

-Jim Otto

~

The true competitors, though, are the ones who always play to win.

-Tom Brady

If I can change then anyone can change. I promise you that.

-Brett Favre

~

Athletic competition
clearly defines the
unique power of our
attitude.

-Bart Starr

You can motivate by fear, and you can motivate by reward. But both those methods are only temporary. The only lasting thing is self motivation.

-Homer Rice

~

What's so wonderful about football and business and show business is that every time I start thinking I'm special, I get knocked on my ass.

-Fran Tarkenton

One man can be a crucial ingredient on a team, but one man cannot make a team.

-Kareem Abdul-Jabbar

~

I like criticism. It makes you strong.

-LeBron James

Success in golf depends less on strength of body than upon strength of mind and character.

-Arnold Palmer

~

When I step on the field, it's on. I know it's time to go to work.

-Ray Lewis

YOU'VE GOT TO STAND UP AND DO YOUR OWN BATTLES. MY DADDY TAUGHT ME THAT A LONG TIME AGO, THAT YOU FIGHT YOUR OWN BATTLES. THE ONLY WAY TO SHUT EVERYBODY UP IS TO WIN.

-TERRY BRADSHAW

~

Be cocky. Walk into the Georgia Dome like you own it.

-Mary Lou Retton

How you recover from what life's throwing at you is what matters.

–Joe Namath

~

Mentally, the only players who survive in the pros are the ones able to manage all their responsibilities. Everybody struggles in different ways.

–Tom Brady

Show me a guy who's afraid to look bad, and I'll show you a guy you can beat every time.

-Lou Brock

~

Set your goals high, and don't stop till you get there.

-Bo Jackson

The hardest skill to acquire in this sport is the one where you compete all out, give it all you have, and you are still getting beat no matter what you do. When you have the killer instinct to fight through that, it is very special.

-Eddie Reese

~

If you step on people in this life, you're going to come back as a cockroach.

-Willie Davis

Good is not good when better
is expected.

-Vin Scully

~

Being thrown into the fire and getting the thing turned around in a hurry made it more difficult. Things have been done the hard way. I think you learn better when things are done the hard way.

-John Elway

You have to be able to accept failure to get better.

-LeBron James

~

I was saying earlier that it's really strange - you can almost step outside yourself and observe yourself running, and that's what I was doing.

-Marcus Allen

I don't want to play golf. When I hit a ball, I want someone else to go chase it.

-Rogers Hornsby

~

Achievements on the golf course are not what matters, decency and honesty are what matter.-

Tiger Woods

Winning is habit.
Unfortunately, so is
losing.

-Vince Lombardi

~

If you don't have
confidence, you'll
always find a way not
to win.

-Carl Lewis

You hope in this life that you grow and don't always repeat your mistakes.

-Tony Dorsett

~

Before we can talk about a championship, we have to practice like a championship team.

-Mike Singletary

I always felt that my
greatest asset was
not my physical
ability, it was my
mental ability.

-Bruce Jenner

~

I think I have a passion for playing the game. I love to play, and I want to play at a high level. You have to do the right things in order to continue at that level.

-Dan Marino

The road to success
is always under
construction.

-Arnold Palmer

~

The principle is competing

against yourself. It's about

self-improvement, about being

better than you were the day

before.

-Steve Young

Your job as a baseball player is to come to the park ready to play every day, and the manager, it's his job to make those decisions about who plays.

-Cal Ripken, Jr.

~

Tennis is a perfect combination of violent action taking place in an atmosphere of total tranquility.

-Billie Jean King

It's hard to win in the NFL. You have to maintain a very delicate balance putting together the right team to be able to win and have any amount of success.

-Barry Sanders

~

If you accept the expectations of others, especially negative ones, then you never will change the outcome.

-Michael Jordan

I believe greatness is an evolutionary process that changes and evolves era to era.

-Michael Jordan

~

Quarterbacks need to make their team better. If it's a bad team, they can even make a bad team better.

-Fran Tarkenton

Most people give up just when they're about to achieve success. They quit on the one yard line. They give up at the last minute of the game one foot from a winning touchdown.

-Ross Perot

~

I think positive. I always think we're going to score.

-Dan Marino

I NEVER COULD STAND LOSING. SECOND PLACE DIDN'T INTEREST ME. I HAD A FIRE IN MY BELLY.

-TY COBB

~

Life is about being a versatile athlete and training in all realms of life.

-Ray Lewis

You can only learn by opening yourself up to engage with different sources of information. How can you learn something if you never see it, read it, or hear it?

-Fran Tarkenton

Always be prepared to start.

Joe Montana

~

I always thought I could play pro ball. I had confidence in my ability, You have to. If you don't who will?

-Johnny Unitas

I think that at some
point in your life
you realize you don't
have to worry if you
do everything you're
supposed to do right.
Or if not right, if
you do it the best
you can... what can
worry do for you? You
are already doing the
best you can.

-Joe Namath

The secret of concentration is the secret of self-discovery. You reach inside yourself to discover your personal resources, and what it takes to match them to the challenge.

-Arnold Palmer

~

Winners, I am convinced, imagine their dreams first. They want it with all their heart and expect it to come true. There is, I believe, no other way to live.

-Joe Montana

When you win, say nothing,

when you lose, say less.

-Paul Brown

~

*Effort without talent is a
depressing situation... but talent
without effort is a tragedy.*

-Mike Ditka

You were born to be a player. You were meant to be here. This moment is yours.

-Herb Brooks

~

The road to success runs uphill.

-Willie Davis

Sports serve society by providing vivid examples of excellence.

-George F. Will

~

Leadership, like coaching, is fighting for the hearts and souls of men and getting them to believe in you.

-Eddie Robinson

You can't be afraid to make errors! You can't be afraid to be naked before the crowd, because no one can ever master the game of baseball, or conquer it. You can only challenge it.

-Lou Brock

~

We all have experiences in our lives that change us, and we all learn from people, like my dad, but at the end of the day, it's only us. And we're only responsible to make ourselves happy.

-Tom Brady

Only he who can see the
invisible can do the
impossible.

-Frank L. Gaines

~

NEVER LET THE FEAR OF STRIKING OUT

GET IN YOUR WAY.

-BABE RUTH

Put your name on something, it better be the best... you only get one shot.

-George Foreman

Anyone can support a team that is winning – it takes no courage. But to stand behind a team to defend a team when it is down and really needs you, that takes a lot of courage.

-Bart Starr

I am building a fire, and everyday I train, I add more fuel. At just the right moment, I light the match.

-Mia Hamm

I think the thing about that was I was always willing to work; I was not the fastest or biggest player but I was determined to be the best football player I could be on the football field and I think I was able to accomplish that through hard work.

-Jerry Rice

If you're afraid to fail, then you're probably going to fail.

-Kobe Bryant

~

Most ball games are lost, not won.

-Casey Stengel

Winning isn't everything, but wanting it is.

-Arnold Palmer

~

You spend a good piece of your life gripping a baseball and in the end it turns out that it was the other way around all the time.

-Jim Bouton

You can't put a limit on anything. The more you dream, the farther you get.

-Michael Phelps

~

If you work harder than somebody else, chances are you'll beat him though he has more talent than you.

-Bart Starr

For athletes, the Olympics are the ultimate test of their worth.

-Mary Lou Retton

~

Champions keep playing until they get it right.

-Billie Jean King

You have to fight to reach your dream. You have to sacrifice and work hard for it.

-Lionel Messi

I don't know why people question the academic training of an athlete. Fifty percent of the doctors in this country graduated in the bottom half of their classes.

-Al McGuire

~

Always make a total effort, even when the odds are against you.

-Arnold Palmer

Without self-discipline,
success is impossible,
period.

-Lou Holtz

~

WHEN YOU HAVE CONFIDENCE, YOU CAN
HAVE A LOT OF FUN. AND WHEN YOU HAVE
FUN, YOU CAN DO AMAZING THINGS.

-JOE NAMATH

~

The only way to prove
that you're a good sport is
to lose.

-Ernie Banks

Everything starts with yourself, with you making up your mind about what you're going to do with your life. I tell kids that it's a cruel world, and that the world will bend them either left or right, and it's up to them to decide which way to bend.

-Tony Dorsett

I think you can be the greatest orator of all time, the greatest motivator of all times, but if those players know that you don't care about them, and you don't try to understand them, then they're never going to hear what you have to say.

–Mike Singletary

If you're not practicing, somebody else is, somewhere, and he'll be ready to take your job.

-Brooks Robinson

~

Most people never run far enough on their first wind to find out they've got a second.

-William James

Some people want it to happen, some wish it would happen, others make it happen.

-Michael Jordan

~

You win some, you lose some, and some get rained out, but you gotta suit up for them all.

-J. Askenberg

Bad attitudes will ruin your team.

-Terry Bradshaw

~

I never looked at the consequences of missing a big shot... when you think about the consequences you always think of a negative result.

-Michael Jordan

The fewer rules a coach has, the fewer rules there are for players to break.

-John Madden

~

It's not the will to win that matters—everyone has that. It's the will to prepare to win that matters.

-Paul "Bear" Bryant

If you can believe it, the mind can achieve it.

-Ronnie Lott

~

I am a winner each and every time I go into the ring.

-George Foreman

Baseball is almost the only orderly thing in a very unorderly world. If you get three strikes, even the best lawyer in the world can't get you off.

-Bill Veeck

~

Many men go fishing all of their lives without knowing that it is not fish they are after.

-Henry David Thoreau

I think the tougher the challenge the better.

-Jim Otto

~

I JUST THINK THAT WE'RE CAPABLE OF SO MUCH MORE; WE DON'T UTILIZE ALL OUR CAPACITY LIKE WE SHOULD.

-MARCUS ALLEN

I never left the field saying
I could have done more to
get ready and that gives
me piece of mind.
-Peyton Manning

When you go out on a football field, you are responsible for taking care of yourself. The more rules you get, the less players truly take care of themselves.

-Jim Brown

I hope the millions of people I've touched have the optimism and desire to share their goals and hard work and persevere with a positive attitude.

-Michael Jordan

I'm not out there sweating for three hours every day just to find out what it feels like to sweat.

-Michael Jordan

~

My approach to every game was to try to erase the games that were before and try to focus on the game at hand.

-Cal Ripken, Jr.

Sometimes you need to get hit in the head to realize that you're in a fight.

-Michael Jordan

~

The triple is the most exciting play in baseball. Home runs win a lot of games, but I never understood why fans are so obsessed with them.

-Hank Aaron

Baseball is a game where a curve is an optical illusion, a screwball can be a pitch or a person, stealing is legal and you can spit anywhere you like except in the umpire's eye or on the ball.

-James Patrick Murray

For every pass I caught in a game, I caught a thousand in practice.

-Don Hutson

~

when you've got
something to prove,
there's nothing
greater than a
challenge.-Terry
Bradshaw

You've got to take the initiative and play your game. In a decisive set, confidence is the difference.

-Chris Evert

~

The plays I remember are the plays I made a mistake.

-Jim Otto

Stubbornness usually is considered a negative; but I think that trait has been a positive for me.

-Cal Ripken Jr.

~

If things came easy, then everybody would be great at what they did, let's face it.

-Mike Ditka

I've learned that something constructive comes from every defeat.

-Tom Landry

~

To succeed, you need to find something to hold on to, something to motivate you, something to inspire you.

-Tony Dorsett

PEOPLE ARE ALWAYS WARNING ME THAT I'M GOING TO BURN OUT. BUT THE TRUTH IS, THE ONLY THING THAT TIRES ME OUT IS HEARING PEOPLE TELL ME THAT. OPPOSITE SHOWS, OPPOSITE COASTS, OPPOSITE DEMOGRAPHICS, OPPOSITE EVERYTHING — I LOVE IT, MAN!

—MICHAEL STRAHAN

My motto was always to keep swinging. Whether I was in a slump or feeling badly or having trouble off the field, the only thing to do was keep swinging.

-Hank Aaron

~

No matter the circumstances that you may be going through, just push through it.

-Ray Lewis

If you ask any great
player or great
quarterback, there's a
certain inner
confidence that you're
as good as anybody. But
you can't say who is the
absolute best. To be
considered is special in
itself.

-Dan Marino

My failures have made me
look at myself in a way I've
never wanted to before.

-Tiger Woods

~

Sports do not build
character. They
reveal it.

-Heywood Broun

The will to win is important, but the will to prepare is vital.

-Joe Paterno

~

Wisdom is always an overmatch for strength.

-Phil Jackson

Gold medals aren't really made of gold. They're made of sweat, determination, and a hard-to-find alloy called guts.

-Dan Gable

~

I never keep a scorecard or the batting averages. I hate statistics. What I got to know, I keep in my head.

-Dizzy Dean

Everything negative -
pressure, challenges
- is all an
opportunity for me to
rise.

-Kobe Bryant

~

**Continuous effort — not strength
or intelligence — is the key to
unlocking our potential.**

-Liane Cardes

You know, heroes are ordinary people that have achieved extraordinary things in life.

-Dave Winfield

~

Just keep going. Everybody gets better if they keep at it.

-Ted Williams

So much of a professional athlete's success depends upon not necessarily the play itself but how he deals with... always saying how you deal with good, is just as important as how you deal with bad.

-Brett Favre

~

Approach the game with no preset agendas and you'll probably come away surprised at your overall efforts.

-Phil Jackson

You are never really playing an opponent. You are playing yourself, your own highest standards, and when you reach your limits, that is real joy.

-Arthur Ashe

When I was 40, my doctor advised me that a man in his 40s shouldn't play tennis. I heeded his advice carefully and could hardly wait until I reached 50 to start again.

–Hugo Black

When you're riding, only the race in which you're riding is important.

-Bill Shoemaker

~

Changing your nature is the hardest thing to do. But I discovered that you can be who you choose to be.

-George Foreman

Just play. Have fun. Enjoy the game.-Michael Jordan

~

Start early and begin raising the bar throughout the day.

-Bruce Jenner

~

There are some things you only learn through experience.

-Joe Namath

Wrestling is ballet with violence.

-Jesse Ventura

~

I think a man becomes less than a man when he begins to compromise on what he believes is right.

-Mike Singletary

I was told I would never make it because I'm too short. Well, I'm still too short. It doesn't matter what your height is, it's what's in your heart.

-Kirby Puckett

~

In life, so many things are taken for granted, but one thing I can honestly say is that I took every day, enjoyed the game of putting on that uniform and playing the great game of baseball.

-Wade Boggs

If you don't think too good,
don't think too much.

-Ted Williams

~

**How you respond to the
challenge in the second half
will determine what you
become after the game,
whether you are a winner or a
loser.**

-Lou Holtz

There comes a time when you have to shut it off, let it go, and say it's not going to happen.

-Art Shell

~

You don't play against opponents, you play against the game of basketball.

-Bobby Knight

I WANT TO RIP OUT HIS HEART AND FEED IT

TO LENNOX LEWIS. I WANT TO KILL

PEOPLE. I WANT TO RIP THEIR STOMACHS

OUT AND EAT THEIR CHILDREN.

-MIKE TYSON

~

I hated every minute of training, but I said, 'Don't quit. Suffer now and live the rest of your life as a champion.

-Muhammad Ali

A man has to have goals – for a day, for a lifetime – and that was mine, to have people say, 'There goes Ted Williams, the greatest hitter who ever lived.'

–Ted Williams

As simple as it sounds, we all must try to be the best person we can: by making the best choices, by making the most of the talents we've been given.

-Mary Lou Retton

~

I believe in being positive.

-Joe Greene

Persistence can
change failure into
extraordinary
achievement.

-Matt Biondi

~

**There is no 'i' in team but
there is in win.**

-Michael Jordan

You always want to
have good balance.
That's the key to
winning a Super Bowl.

-John Elway

~

Your biggest opponent isn't
the other guy. It's human
nature.

-Bobby Knight

Baseball is the only field of endeavor where a man can succeed three times out of ten and be considered a good performer.

-Ted Williams

~

If you have everything under control, you're not moving fast enough.

-Mario Andretti

I was very fortunate to play sports. All the anger in me went out. I had to do what I had to do. If you stay angry all the time, then you really don't have a good life.

-Willie Mays

~

Show me a good loser, and I'll show you a loser.

-Vince Lombardi

If you can maintain that
integrity in whatever you do,
you can't go wrong.

-George Foreman

~

**Life deals you a lot lessons,
some people learn from it, some
people don't.**

-Brett Favre

I don't live in the past.

-Joe Montana

~

Every night on the court I give my all, and if I'm not giving 100 percent, I criticize myself.

-LeBron James

BASEBALL HAS THE GREAT ADVANTAGE
OVER CRICKET OF BEING SOONER ENDED.

-GEORGE BERNARD SHAW

~

You can't win if nobody
catches the ball in the
outfield. You're only as
good as the team you have
behind you.

-Jim Palmer

I learned that if you want to make it bad enough, no matter how bad it is, you can make it.

-Gale Sayers

~

Pressure is something you feel when you don't know what the hell you're doing.

-Peyton Manning

Don't walk through life just playing football. Don't walk through life just being an athlete. Athletics will fade. Character and integrity and really making an impact on someone's life, that's the ultimate vision, that's the ultimate goal - bottom line.

-Ray Lewis

It's just a job. Grass grows, birds fly, waves pound the sand. I beat people up.

-Muhammad Ali

~

I'm a competitive person and I love the challenge of mastering new things.

-Sasha Cohen

There's not anything
I don't think I can
do or accomplish.

-Drew Brees

~

I consider adversity being good

sometimes, you know.

-Brett Favre

Excellence is the gradual result of always striving to do better.

-Pat Riley

~

The ones who want to achieve and win championships motivate themselves.

-Mike Ditka

A pitcher has to look at the hitter as his mortal enemy.

-Early Wynn

~

One man practicing sportsmanship is far better than 50 preaching it.

-Knute Rockne

The integrity of the game is everything.

-Peter Ueberroth

~

Life doesn't run away from nobody. Life runs at people.

-Joe Frazier

Limits, like fear, is often an illusion.

-Michael Jordan

~

As a team, you need to come from behind every once in awhile just to do it. Good for the attitude. It makes it exciting. And when everybody knows you have to throw it... that makes it fun too.

-Dan Marino

WHEN THE GOING GETS WEIRD, THE WEIRD
TURN PRO.

-HUNTER S. THOMPSON

~

You have competition
every day because you set
such high standards for
yourself that you have to
go out every day and live
up to that

·-Michael Jordan

That's my gift. I let that negativity roll off me like water off a duck's back. If it's not positive, I didn't hear it. If you can overcome that, fights are easy.

-George Foreman

You've got to get good habits of working hard so that when that play comes up during the regular season that you're able to complete it and do it the right way.

-Al Kaline

I can accept failure, everyone fails at something. But I can't accept not trying.

-Michael Jordan

~

To be a leader, you have to make people want to follow you, and nobody wants to follow someone who doesn't know where he is going.

-Joe Namath

You can't be afraid to fail. It's the only way you succeed.

LeBron James

You know, I think when I reflect on it, I think there's certainly a sense of history. When you have ambitions to play this game, you want to be one of the best ever, and you want to play so well and be so effective that you want people to remember your name 100 years from now.

-Marcus Allen

Vision gets the dreams started. Dreaming employs your God-given imagination to reinforce the vision. Both are part of something I believe is absolutely necessary to building the life of a champion, a winner, a person of high character who is consistently at the top of whatever game he or she is in.

-Emmitt Smith

To uncover your true potential you must first find your own limits and then you have to have the courage to blow past them.

-Picabo Street

~

Everyone wants to beat us. So you can never take a single game lightly.

-Jim Otto

You got to be willing to walk in a storm. That's what I tell people all the time.

-Ray Lewis

~

As simple as it sounds, we all must try to be the best person

We can: by making the best choices, by making the most of the talents we've been given.

-Mary Lou Retton

There's one secret to hitting hard, and that is to completely dedicate your body. That's the difference between a man going forward and a man going backward, no matter how big he is.

-Ray Lewis

Cause there's only one reason for doing anything that you set out to do. If you don't want to be the best, then there's no reason going out and trying to accomplish anything.

-Joe Montana

The difference between the old ballplayer and the new ballplayer is the jersey. The old ballplayer cared about the name on the front. The new ballplayer cares about the name on the back.

-Steve Garvey

You find that you have peace of mind and can enjoy yourself, get more sleep, and rest when you know that it was a one hundred percent effort that you gave—win or lose.

-Gordie Howe

~

I'm tired of hearing about money, money, money, money, money. I just want to play the game, drink Pepsi, wear Reebok.

-Shaquille O'Neal

Some people take certain things and they try to forget what that pain felt like. I don't. I take that same pain and I chase it every time I walk in a weight room.

-Ray Lewis

~

I was a workhorse; there was never a practice that I didn't enjoy.

-Joe Namath

SUCCESS IS WHERE PREPARATION AND
OPPORTUNITY MEET.

-BOBBY UNSER

~

I became a good pitcher
when I stopped trying to
make them miss the ball
and started trying to make
them hit it.

-Sandy Koufax

One thing that I don't think my critics realize about me is that I've been trained to look adversity in the face.

-Reggie White

~

A lifetime of training for just ten seconds.

-Jesse Owens

The more difficult the victory,
the greater the happiness in
winning.

-Pele

~

If at first you don't
succeed, you are
running about
average.

-M.H. Alderson

**Push yourself again and again.
Don't give an inch until the
final buzzer sounds.**

-Larry Bird

~

Never give up, never
give in, and when the
upper hand is ours,
may we have the
ability to handle the
win with the dignity
that we absorbed the
loss.

-Doug Williams

I want to be remembered like Pete Rose. 'Charlie Hustle.' I want people to say, 'Wherever he was, he was always giving it his all.'

-Walter Payton

~

I've always believed that if you put in the work, the results will come.

-Michael Jordan

Do you know what my favorite part of the game is? The opportunity to play.

-Mike Singletary

~

Dreaming means 'rehearsing' what you see, playing it over and over in your mind until it becomes as real to you as your life right now.

-Emmitt Smith

You cannot allow your desire to be a winner to be diminished by achieving success before and I believe there is room for improvement in every sportsman.

-Lionel Messi

~

In any team sport, the best teams have consistency and chemistry.

-Roger Staubach

If football taught me anything about business, it is that you win the game one play at a time.

-Fran Tarkenton

~

I don't care to be remembered as the man who scored six touchdowns in a game. I want to be remembered as a winner in life.

-Gale Sayers

If you wait for the right time or the good times to start a business, you wait all your life.

Fran Tarkenton

~

SOMEBODY WILL ALWAYS BREAK YOUR RECORDS. IT IS HOW YOU LIVE THAT COUNTS.

-EARL CAMPBELL

I don't need to be motivated by anybody. Never have.

-Dan Marino

~

I was doing what I love to do: play baseball. Not going to complain about that.

-Willie McCovey

My motto was always to keep swinging. Whether I was in a slump or feeling badly or having trouble off the field, the only thing to do was keep swinging.

Hank Aaron

I don't think about goals and records. Competition is what keeps me playing.

-Lou Brock

~

I wouldn't say anything is impossible. I think that everything is possible as long as you put your mind to it and put the work and time into it.

-Michael Phelps

The difference between the impossible and the possible lies in a person's determination.

-Tommy Lasorda

~

There is no such thing as a perfect basketball player, and I don't believe there is only one greatest player either.

-Michael Jordan

More enduringly than any other sport, wrestling teaches self-control and pride. Some have wrestled without great skill - none have wrestled without pride.

-Dan Gable

~

Confidence comes from hours and days and weeks and years of constant work and dedication.

-Roger Staubach

Steroids are for guys who want to cheat opponents.

-Lawrence Taylor

~

A trophy carries dust. Memories last forever.

-Mary Lou Retton

It's all about putting the best team together - not just in the front office but the players on the field.

-John Elway

~

You wouldn't have won if we'd beaten you.

-Yogi Berra

When you are not practicing, someone else is getting better.

-Allen Iverson

~

Too often in life, something happens and we blame other people for us not being happy or satisfied or fulfilled. So the point is, we all have choices, and we make the choice to accept people or situations or to not accept situations.

-Tom Brady

I can't relate to lazy people. We don't speak the same language. I don't understand you. I don't want to understand you.

-Kobe Bryant

~

WHEN YOU LOSE, THERE IS A WHOLE BUNCH OF ROOM FOR NEGATIVITY AND I DON'T FEED INTO THIS STUFF AND I DO NOT DO ANY TALKING.

-ALLEN IVERSON

During my 18 years I came to bat almost 10,000 times. I struck out about 1,700 times and walked maybe 1,800 times. You figure a ballplayer will average about 500 at bats a season. That means I played seven years without ever hitting the ball.

-Mickey Mantle

Obstacles don't have to stop you. If you run into a wall, don't turn around and give up. Figure out how to climb it, go through it, or work around it.

-Michael Jordan

Fans don't boo nobodies.

−Reggie Jackson

~

Somewhere behind the athlete you've become and the hours of practice and the coaches who have pushed you is a little girl who fell in love with the game and never looked back... play for her.

-Mia Hamm

An athlete cannot run with money in his pockets. He must run with hope in his heart and dreams in his head.

-Emil Zatopek

~

Whether it's 18 years old or 40 years old, we think we know what's going on. But if you're lucky enough to continue the journey, it's amazing how we keep learning how much we didn't know.

-Joe Namath

You can do more, you
can always do more.

-Dan Marino

~

You have to be like a clock

spring, wound but not loose at

the same time.

-Dave Winfield

Talent wins games, but teamwork and intelligence wins championships.

-Michael Jordan

~

It ain't over till it's over.

-Yogi Berra

I want to be perceived as a guy who played his best in all facets, not just scoring. A guy who loved challenges.

-Michael Jordan

~

Nobody's a natural. You work hard to get good and then work to get better. It's hard to stay on top.

-Paul Coffey

Always turn a negative
situation into a positive
situation.

-Michael Jordan

~

**What to do with a mistake:
recognize it, admit it, learn from
it, forget it.**

-Dean Smith

To me, it didn't matter where I played,
I just wanted to play well.

-Ronnie Lott

~

The only way to prove that
you're a good sport is to
lose.

-Ernie Banks

PEOPLE WANT A COP-OUT, LISTEN I'M A REALIST AND I TALK ABOUT MOTIVATION, TALK ABOUT ALL THE THINGS IT TAKES TO BE GREATER OR ARE IMPORTANT TO WIN AND PEOPLE WANT TO USE EXCUSES ALL THE TIME.

-MIKE DITKA

Every quarterback can throw a ball; every running back can run; every receiver is fast; but that mental toughness that you talk about translates into competitiveness.

-Tom Brady

You can't win unless you learn how to lose. - Kareem

Abdul-Jabbar

~

Do not let what you cannot do interfere with what you can do.

-John Wooden

Be true to the game,
because the game will
be true to you. If
you try to shortcut
the game, then the
game will shortcut
you. If you put forth
the effort, good
things will be
bestowed upon you.
That's truly about
the game, and in some
ways that's about
life too.

-Michael Jordan

I am not too serious about anything. I believe you have to enjoy yourself to get the most out of your ability. I can take the criticism with the accolades. Neither affects me.

-George Brett

~

You can always be a little bit better.

-Drew Brees

Winners live in the present tense. People who come up short are consumed with future or past. I want to be living in the now.

-Alex Rodriguez

~

I have a memory, and I can just eliminate mistakes when they come up because I've already made them.

-Tom Brady

Our lives are not
determined by what
happens to us but how
we react to what
happens, not by what
life brings us but
the attitude we bring
to life.

-Wade Boggs

~

**The five S's of sports training are:
stamina, speed, strength, skill,
and spirit; but the greatest of
these is spirit.**

-Ken Doherty

A champion is someone who gets up when he can't.

-Jack Dempsey

~

If you got the game, you got the game. That's why Tiger Woods is out there playing golf with Greg Norman.

~Shaquille O'Neal

There are only two options regarding commitment. You're either IN or you're OUT. There is no such thing as life in-between.

-Pat Riley

~

I had one of my best years in 1991; I was 31. I made a renewed effort to work harder. I got better at my diet. I paid attention to how much sleep I got. I was always someone of routine. I became more strict.

-Cal Ripken, Jr.

Number one is just to gain a passion for running. To love the morning, to love the trail, to love the pace on the track. And if some kid gets really good at it, that's cool too.

-Pat Tyson

~

IF YOU ARE DETERMINED ENOUGH AND WILLING TO PAY THE PRICE, YOU CAN GET IT DONE.

-MIKE DITKA

I've experienced the highest of highs and lowest of lows. I think to really appreciate anything you have to be at both ends of the spectrum.

-John Elway

~

Demand excellence.

-Emmitt Smith

Sure, the home-field is an advantage - but so is having a lot of talent.

-Dan Marino

~

I spent twelve years training for a career that was over in a week. Joe Namath spent one week training for a career that lasted twelve years.

-Bruce Jenner

I've never been afraid to fail.

-Michael Jordan

~

If I'm going to play, it's going to be 100-percent commitment.

-Brett Favre

I couldn't do anything I didn't enjoy.

-Joe Namath

~

You need to feel that the game is important to you. Lose that feeling and you lose your edge. There's no faking that kind of emotion. You can't invent the feeling. It's got to be natural, real.

-Dan Marino

I always had the attitude that I wanted to throw a no-hitter every game.

-Dennis Eckersley

~

What makes something special is not just what you have to gain, but what you feel there is to lose.

-Andre Agassi

A good hockey player plays where the puck is. A great hockey player plays where the puck is going to be.

-Wayne Gretzky

~

People ask me what I do in winter when there's no baseball. I'll tell you what I do. I stare out the window and wait for spring.

-Rogers Hornsby

I get up in the morning looking for an adventure.

-George Foreman

~

I play to win, whether during practice or a real game. And I will not let anything get in the way of me and my competitive enthusiasm to win.

-Michael Jordan

For me, winning isn't something that happens suddenly on the field when the whistle blows and the crowds roar. Winning is something that builds physically and mentally every day that you train and every night that you dream.

-Emmitt Smith

YOU HAVE TO STAY ONE LEVEL ABOVE
EVERYONE ELSE.

-JIM OTTO

~

Age is no barrier. It's a limitation you put on your mind.

-Jackie Joyner-Kersee

When the year starts the objective is to win it all with the team, personal records are secondary.

-Lionel Messi

The mind is the limit.
As long as the mind
can envision the fact
that you can do
something, you can do
it, as long as you really
believe 100 percent.

-Arnold
Schwarzenegger

Enjoy your sweat because hard work doesn't guarantee success, but without it you don't have a chance.

-Alex Rodriguez

~

If you fail to prepare, you're prepared to fail.- Mark Spitz

It's a round ball and a round bat, and you got to hit it square.

-Pete Rose

Stealing bases was put to me almost as a prerequisite for staying in the game. They didn't give me a handbook on how to do it; they said do it. Under those conditions you go out and develop your own handbook.

-Lou Brock

I think that at the start of a game, you're always playing to win, and then maybe if you're ahead late in the game, you start playing not to lose. The true competitors, though, are the ones who always play to win.

-Tom Brady

Never give up! Failure and rejection are only the first step to succeeding.

-Jim Valvano

~

When I go out there, I have no pity on my brother. I am out there to win.

-Joe Frazier

Adversity cause some
men to break; others
to break records.

-William A. Ward

~

**Losing is no disgrace if you've
given your best.**

-Jim Palmer

My mom is real passionate and a family-first woman. She always told me that just because I can shoot a basketball better than someone else, I shouldn't think that I'm better than them.

–Derrick Rose

~

The road to Easy Street goes through the sewer.

-John Madden

If you aren't going all the way, why go at all?

-Joe Namath

~

Our young people look up to us. Let us not let them down. Our young people need us. Saving them will make heroes of us all.

-Gale Sayers

I like added pressure. It makes me work harder.

-Mary Lou Retton

~

YOU HAVE TO PLAY WITH THE MENTALITY THAT YOU ARE ABOUT TO LOSE YOUR JOB, AND THAT THEY'RE GOING TO TALK ABOUT 'THE OTHER GUY' FIRST. YOU HAVE TO THINK, 'I WANT MY NAME MENTIONED FIRST.'

-BRETT FAVRE

You have to expect things of yourself before you can do them.

-Michael Jordan

~

Nothing good comes in life or athletics unless a lot of hard work has preceded the effort. Only temporary success is achieved by taking short cuts.

-Roger Staubach

Conceit is bragging about yourself. Confidence means you believe you can get the job done.

–Johnny Unitas

~

Bulls do not win bull fights. People do.

-Norman Ralph Augustine

You always get a special kick on opening day, no matter how many you go through. You look forward to it like a birthday party when you're a kid. You think something wonderful is going to happen.
-Joe DiMaggio

~

Winning isn't getting ahead of others. It's getting ahead of yourself.

-Roger Staubach

All camps are hard,
that's what they're
intended to be. They
make you focus when
you're tired, when
you don't feel like
doing things, and to
see how long you can
retain and pay
attention.

-Michael Strahan

What you lack in talent can be made up with desire, hustle, and giving 1 10 percent all the time.

-Don Zimmer

~

Success isn't permanent and failure isn't fatal.

-Mike Ditka

If you can't outplay them, outwork them.

-Ben Hogan

~

The team that is the most focused and executes the best is the team that wins. That's usually the team that can handle the pressure of the situation.

-Michael Strahan

I have a message for the young kids. Life is about obstacles, endeavors in life are not to be overlooked.

-Wade Boggs

~

One of life's most painful moments comes when we must admit that we didn't do our homework, that we are not prepared.

-Merlin Olsen

Every day when I get on the floor I give it my all and play because you never know what tomorrow holds.

-Russell Westbrook

~

Every great batter works on the theory that the pitcher is more afraid of him than he is of the pitcher.

-Ty Cobb

The highest compliment
that you can pay me is to
say that I work hard every
day, that I never dog it.

-Wayne Gretzky

~

TO ME IT WAS NEVER ABOUT WHAT I

ACCOMPLISHED ON THE FOOTBALL FIELD,

IT WAS ABOUT THE WAY I PLAYED THE

GAME.

-JERRY RICE

Success is measured by your discipline and inner peace.

-Mike Ditka

~

It's not that difficult to win. It's more difficult to win consistently and stay on top.

-Jim Otto

My mother and father, Joe and Theresa Montana brought me along and taught me to never quit, and to strive to be the best.

–Joe Montana

I think goals should never be easy, they should force you to work, even if they are uncomfortable at the time.

-Michael Phelps

~

I had to fight all my life to survive. They were all against me... but I beat the bastards and left them in the ditch.

-Ty Cobb

Win If You Can, Lose If You Must, But NEVER QUIT!

-Cameron Trammell

~

You learn a lot more from the lows because it makes you pay attention to what you're doing.

-John Elway

Hitting is timing. Pitching is upsetting timing.

-Warren Spahn

~

When I lose the sense of motivation and the sense to prove something as a basketball player, it's time for me to move away from the game.

-Michael Jordan

A positive attitude causes a chain reaction of positive thoughts, events and outcomes. It is a catalyst and it sparks extraordinary results.

-Wade Boggs

~

If winning isn't everything, why do they keep score?

-Vince Lombardi

I've figured out that life in general is a team effort; it's a team game.

-Joe Namath

~

You must play boldly to win.

-Arnold Palmer

Nobody who ever gave his best regretted it.

-George Halas

~

Make each day your masterpiece.

-John Wooden

In order to excel, you must be completely dedicated to your chosen sport. You must also be prepared to work hard and be willing to accept constructive criticism. Without one-hundred percent dedication, you won't be able to do this.

-Willie Mays

I THINK EVERY PLAYER SHOULD THINK THAT
HE'S A DIFFERENCE MAKER

-BRETT FAVRE

~

I'm never satisfied. I'm always trying to get better and learn from my mistakes.

-Russell Westbrook

I always want to win
because I never want to
sit out on the sidelines
outside.

-Kevin Durant

11278969R00114

Printed in Great Britain
by Amazon.co.uk, Ltd.,
Marston Gate.